W9-AJM-231

STAR WARS™

Grogu's Galaxy

DK
Senior Editor Matt Jones
Project Art Editor Chris Gould
Production Editor Marc Staples
Senior Production Controller Mary Slater
Managing Editor Emma Grange
Managing Art Editor Vicky Short
Publishing Director Mark Searle

Designed for DK by Sandra Perry
Reading Consultant Barbara Marinak

For Lucasfilm
Senior Editor Brett Rector
Creative Director, Publishing Michael Siglain
Art Director Troy Alders
Story Group Leland Chee, Pablo Hidalgo, and Kate Izquierdo
Creative Art Manager Phil Szostak

Asset Management Sarah Williams, Elinor De La Torre, Jackey Cabrera, Bryce Pinkos, Erik Sanchez, and Shahana Alam

DK would like to thank Chelsea Alon and Krista Wong at Disney; and Julia March and Megan Douglass for proofreading.

First American Edition, 2023
Published in the United States by DK Publishing
1745 Broadway, 20th Floor, New York, NY 10019

Page design copyright © 2023 Dorling Kindersley Limited
DK, a Division of Penguin Random House LLC

© & TM 2023 LUCASFILM LTD

23 24 25 26 27 10 9 8 7 6 5 4 3 2 1
001–333493–Mar/2023

All rights reserved.
Without limiting the rights under the copyright reserved above, no part of this publication may be reproduced, stored in or introduced into a retrieval system, or transmitted, in any form, or by any means (electronic, mechanical, photocopying, recording, or otherwise), without the prior written permission of the copyright owner.
Published in Great Britain by Dorling Kindersley Limited

A catalog record for this book is available from the Library of Congress.
ISBN 978-0-7440-7065-1 (Paperback)
ISBN 978-0-7440-7066-8 (Hardcover)

DK books are available at special discounts when purchased in bulk for sales promotions, premiums, fund-raising, or educational use.
For details, contact: DK Publishing Special Markets, 1745 Broadway, 20th Floor, New York, NY 10019
SpecialSales@dk.com

Printed and bound in China

For the curious

www.dk.com
www.starwars.com

MIX
Paper | Supporting responsible forestry
FSC™ C018179
FSC
www.fsc.org

This book was made with Forest Stewardship Council ™ certified paper—one small step in DK's commitment to a sustainable future.
For more information go to www.dk.com/our-green-pledge

Level 1

STAR WARS™

Grogu's Galaxy

Matt Jones

DK

Contents

6 Grogu
8 The Mandalorian
10 The Force
12 Grogu and the Force
14 Kuiil
16 Grogu's pram
18 Peli Motto
20 Hungry Grogu
22 Ahsoka Tano
24 Zooming ship
26 Luke Skywalker
28 Great team

30 Glossary
31 Index
32 Quiz

Grogu

Say hello to Grogu. Grogu is from another galaxy.

Grogu cares about his friends.

The Mandalorian

The Mandalorian is called Din Djarin. He is Grogu's friend.

Din keeps Grogu safe.

The Force

The Force is a powerful energy. Some people use the Force to do great things.

Grogu and the Force

Grogu can use the Force. He can use it to put creatures to sleep.

Rancor

Kuiil

Kuiil lives on the planet Arvala-7. He likes to fix machines.

Kuiil helps Din and Grogu to repair their starship.

Grogu's pram

Grogu has a special pram.
It can float in the air.

His friend Kuiil made it for him.

Peli Motto

Peli Motto is one of Grogu's friends. She loves taking care of Grogu.

Grogu and Peli have lots of fun together.

Hungry Grogu

Grogu gets hungry very often.
He likes to try different types of food.

Soup

Squid

Cookie

Spider eggs

Ahsoka Tano

Ahsoka Tano is a smart hero.

She can use the Force. Grogu meets Ahsoka on the planet Corvus.

Zooming ship

Grogu enjoys it when starships move really fast.

He gets very excited.

Luke Skywalker

Luke Skywalker is a Jedi.
Jedi can use the Force
to help people.
Luke teaches Grogu
about the Force.

Great team

Grogu and Din are a great team. They visit many planets together.

Glossary

galaxy
a large group of stars and planets

pram
another word for a baby carriage

rancor
a type of creature

repair
mending something that is broken

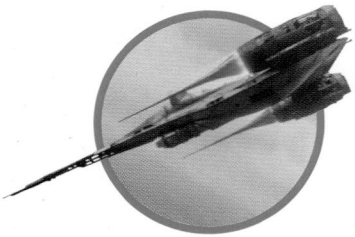

starship
a type of ship used to travel in space

Index

Ahsoka Tano 22–23
Arvala-7 14
Corvus 23
Din Djarin 8–9, 15, 28
food 20, 21
Force, the 10–11, 12, 23, 26
galaxy 6
Grogu 6–7, 8, 9, 12, 15, 16, 18, 19, 20–21, 23, 24, 26, 28
Jedi 26
Kuiil 14–15, 17
Luke Skywalker 26–27
Mandalorian, the 8–9
Peli Motto 18–19
pram 16
rancor 13
starship 15, 24

Quiz

Ready to find out how much you have learned? Read the questions and then check your answers with an adult.

1. Is Luke Skywalker a Jedi?
2. Who repairs Din and Grogu's starship?
3. Where does Ahsoka Tano meet Grogu?
4. What is the Mandalorian's name?
5. Can Grogu use the Force?

1. Yes 2. Kuiil 3. The planet Corvus 4. Din Djarin 5. Yes